MW00625918

THE RENTED ALTAR

LAUREN BERRY

POETRY

C&R Press
Conscious & Responsible

C&R Press
Conscious & Responsible
crpress.org

For special discounted bulk purchases, please contact:
C&R Press sales@crpress.org
Contact info@crpress.org to book events, readings and author signings.

THE RENTED ALTAR

TABLE OF CONTENTS

ENGAGEMENT

HONEYMOON

LABOR

SPLINTER

ENGAGEMENT

Dunedin, Florida

1019 MYRTLE FURROW LANE

Because the threshold had already been crossed by his first wife,
        I investigated each room with wonder, pretending I was

touring a freshly burned down museum. I searched for what I wanted
        to keep, what I wanted to release, and what I wanted to build again

with my own hands. I imagined I was fire. I touched everything.
        I pressed my ear to the floors that supported his first wife's feet

as they slowly kissed in the kitchen or argued about religion in the hall.
        When I caressed the walls with my husband's paint brush, the house

warmed to me. It said, *Enter.* It said, *I'm yours now.* Or was it, *For now?*
        Could the house have imagined it would host another bride?

I picture the first wife up against the bedroom window, pregnant
        and trembling under the white ceiling she found so blinding

that she painted it with two coats of midnight blue. What did she know then
        that made her dim the room where they made him?

THE EVER AFTER BRIDAL STORE

The saleswoman's skin
was tan as my mother's
when she held that white lace
high above my head

but it wasn't.
The way I hid my breasts
in the chipped-paint
dressing room
was like standing in front
of my childhood

pediatrician but it wasn't.
The saleswoman ran
that zipper up my back
and it was like the doctor's
dry finger as it hunted

scoliosis. The Greek word
for "broken" rushed to my head
like blood as I bent over
wondering if I could spell it.

But I couldn't. But it
wasn't. And now I think
the pink tape measure,
glossy around my hips,
might have been a kind

of diagnosis but was it?
When my girlfriends sipped their
drugstore champagne
in the plastic red cups from
the bridal store's back room,

they looked pretty as my sisters
and they were the same in number
and they were patient as when

we waited our turn
to learn about our own
tiny spines. Were we broken
or weren't we? But we aren't.

MY FIANCE'S FIRST WIFE SEWS LINGERIE
FOR MY WEDDING NIGHT

Every Tuesday night
she disrobes me on her deck
with her mouth full of thread.

It's a faintly lit heaven,
so much like the screened-in porch
of their first house
where she slept when pregnant
and feeling as caged in
as a body in black mesh.

In silence, she measures
my shoulders, shakes
her head at their narrowness.
She slits open

a package of needles
and lets me choose
which one she will use.

His first wife begins
by boiling thread in a cup
of her boy's bathwater
until it hisses. She flattens

her hand across the mouth
of the pot like she might
tame the first vapor that rises.

His first wife unfolds
a ream of black silk so delicate
it can turn back into worms
if you talk bad about her.

Where a fur-lined collar might be,
she weaves locks of her blond hair
with mine. For the garter belt,

she stains a ribbon of satin
with the burgundy lipstick
she smeared on for a photo
the night their son was born.

In place of a corset, a fence
of warped plastic forks
from her son's first birthday.

From nursery rhymes sliced
out of the boy's first book,
she crafts a series of paper veils.

Or maybe they're blindfolds.
Someone will have to lead me
to the bed. When I try one on,

all I see are the words she sang
to her son at the end
of each day— the story

about the baby
in a little cradle
who, one evening, fell.

Each time I leave
his first wife's house,
some shadow, some
silent armor, some
blueprint of myself
stays behind.

The rest of me ignites
in her doorway as I whisk
a disk of cinnamon
from her candy dish

and whip it into my mouth
but it never lasts. No matter
how fast I beat back
to her first husband
the heat always dissolves
before I can get to him.

THE RENTED ALTAR

I suppose I am blessed enough.
Most of what I love finds a way

to love me back. And yet,
the day after our wedding,
the entire town comes down

with fever. I check my forehead
and the path where I stood alone
for portraits. My mother rushed

to adjust the hem of my dress into a circle
as perfect as a wedding band.
That grass is now a ring of yellow blades.

The first morning of my marriage
I found my husband on the floor,
my dress collapsed beneath him.

The delicate glass that we raised
during my father's champagne toast
smashed to pieces on the road
I now wake up on.

I knew this would happen.
Even when I love as well as I can,
I leave a wake of ruin.

Even now the backyard garden gate
where I promised to die
before I'd leave my husband
ensnares in kudzu vines.

The painted sign that directed guests
to our ceremony chokes in thorns,
our names hidden under barbs.

With white cake still glowing
in their stomachs, my sisters whisper
about where the rented altar went
but I'm afraid to answer.

I can still see my mother lunging
at my feet with her clicking manicure,
how she backed away from me
with her palms covering her face
as though I were on fire.

VOW IN WHICH WE TIE OUR HANDS BEHIND OUR BACKS

Last night we argued
over who is in charge
of hunger. Who leads
the sheets to twist
and at which thigh?

We bickered
in lamplight. I said
I wished to drink
the bitter of his body.
He said he wished
the bitter of mine.

On our knees we are
anvils, engraved
with submissive logic.

With anyone else,
we match. We prizefight,
we bout, we contest.

With each other,
we cannot protest.
We have no fists.

I kneel in praise of him.
I bow, he taunts me.
He kneels in praise of me.
He bows, I taunt him.

The priest who married us
modeled how to lift our chins,
part our lips to Christ's body

but who is the savior?
Who is the saved?
Who will get us out of here
when we have no savage left?

THE GAME OF MAKE-BELIEVE

Never in my childhood did I pretend I was a bride.
As a girl, I lined plastic horses into strict parades
under my mother as she ironed her spouse's shirts

to a crisp. I bound glossy stallions in chains as they pranced
in tandem through a kingdom where I was Queen. I practiced
the perfect wave with a sash across my heart. But never

was there a King in the carriage. Never a male heir
revealed to paparazzi. When I held my mother's heels, I ran
a finger over their spikes. As that child, I bathed for hours.

I pretended I was the most tragic of all mermaids, kidnapped
by an evil circus ringleader. He sold tickets to men who begged me
to flap my emerald tail, splash their faces with icy water.

When I slid back the shower curtain, I held a red and gold fold
of the big top in my fist. I could hold my breath forever,
which I needed when I became a runaway in the swamps,

riding alligator minions through the creeks, fireflies in our wake.
I trained blue herons to braid my hair into mazes with their beaks.
My armies of shadow children crafted tents with coyote bones, devised

plans to capture territory. Before war, they rolled out a carpet
of moss. Was it the aisle that led me to my husband? The one
I love above any other creation. The one I did not will into being.

WHITE PICKET FENCE AND BLACK COFFEE

I can no longer rely on my dreams | but I can still taste | the metallic mouth |
of his silver |coffee carafe | how black water rose out of it | crept |

along the hardwoods | where we had just | buttoned our white shirts | and stood up |
The water swelled | toward me | I questioned | how much I had poured

into its blessed cavern | I confess | I had welcomed | its aromatic hush | of black sand
| distracting | and impossible to measure | so much like the dry shore

of my home |but I tell you now | water overflowed the vessel | drowned the floor
biblically |with boiling water | I yelled | *I can't stop it!* | but the darkness met me

like doubt | burned my toes | my ankles | my knees | my thighs | my hips| breasts
were on fire but the water | never lightened | never cooled |I told him

I am going |*to drown here* | In the black water swirled swarms |of wedding rings |
swirled | lace-trimmed photo albums | swirled | a young boy | swirled| an untamed

garden | the door to our house| my reflection| warped by the water | and from the stairwell
| he said | *Just leave it* | *my wife* | *will fix it* |*when she returns* |

.

HONEYMOON

HONEYMOON ISLAND

Perhaps it was for the best that we never planned a honeymoon.

After the last dance, we just went home and folded
my gown into a cardboard box. Like a child, I peered in

the freezer's silver mist, slid slices of our coconut cake inside.
My new husband unhooked my hundred satin buttons

while humming a tune I'd never heard before.
He washed my face and then his own with the same bar of soap.

He kissed me. I was home. That night I dreamt of Honeymoon Island, a key
of land sheared off by a hurricane. In 1939, a millionaire

built fifty thatched huts along the shore for newlyweds.
When I woke, I asked my husband if the lucky brides' moans

traveled to meet waves as they crested. Did the grooms shave
their mustaches with ocean water, the salt sting waking them up

from their haze? That first month, my husband and I went nowhere.
I grew restless in our brick house, changed all its switches and knobs,

counted the swinging hangers in all five of our closets, rearranged
pregnancy tests by color. By price. By name. I fed my husband

and his son honey at every meal. I drizzled flower patterns
onto their vanilla yogurt, their burnt barbeque chicken, their

peanut butter banana sandwiches sliced by his first wife's knife which
I was still getting used to. I filled their teacups with gold.

Their blood sugar soared. They grew lethargic in the evenings.
While they dozed on our couches, I sat in a ring of encyclopedias, paged

through honeymoon history, tracking details with a sharpened pencil, scratching
them onto crisp index cards that during the day I hid in a box

of tampons. In Norse, the word for honeymoon means "in hiding."
Legend has it that a man would kidnap a woman, keep her unseen

until her clan gave up the search. Or she became pregnant
with a new god and no one could dispute the union. Honeymoon.

The night of our wedding, I bled carnations onto our sheets.

THE SAME SCRAWLED QUESTION

When the doorknob yields to my husband's twist, I am on my back

on our hardwood floor, half-crab and half-woman, a tangle
of expectation strangled across my chest like gray netting. The sour ruin

of saltwater in my mouth does not rush its flavor; it turns me

over and over as I claw my way to him. Each scratch on the floor
is the same scrawled question: *What is it, what is it, what is it*

a wife is supposed to do for her husband at the end of each day?

WHERE MY MIND WENT DURING THE FIRST ULTRASOUND

Because I couldn't read
the screen to know
the plot of that silent film,

I pictured my womb
as a living room at dusk
in a Victorian orphanage.

Every wall was mahogany.
Every wall was engraved
with angels carved by a god
skilled but unanswerable,

mysterious as my unborn children
who lived there... who threw dice,
solved riddles, spun stories of rescue
in front of a fireplace that crackled,
burned their sheet music until
it was unrecognizable. The flames

crisped branches too, ivory
kindling from the forest they know
better than to enter alone.

They didn't look up
when I called to them.
They made their own joy.

When it was time, my sons
carried my daughters to bed
where they recited
the Lord's prayer twice
and tucked themselves
under sheets of white lace

in the part of my body
that no one, not even
this music can reach.

THE BAR OF DOVE SOAP HIS FIRST WIFE LEFT BEHIND

I refused to bathe
when I first moved in.

I'd lock the door and just
sit in the belly
of the porcelain tub,
whispering to her
white bar of soap.

I'd say things like,
"This is where she soaked
with my stepson
glittering inside her.

Look at you, little soul.
You were never meant
to have your own authority,
unaware even of the one word
carved into your body,

or the image of a bird
without permission
to beat its wings.

My husband's first wife
held you to her fluttering,
broken heart. You

couldn't match it. He
couldn't match it. I
can't match it. You

sour into a muted gray,
moaning for the curve
under her arms, the warmth
between her legs.

When I lift you
to my lips, your scent
doesn't rise, doesn't clean
this stain. Can't you just
pretend I'm her?"

MY HUSBAND PRESSES MY CHEEK AGAINST
THE BEDROOM WALL'S WET PAINT

I'd seen it done before
with a newborn's hands
at the hospital
named for a saint.

The child was not in the world
an hour before there was
dark ink at the ends of her

ten fingers and the feet
she'd one day use to walk
out of her father's house.

The doctor captured her
labyrinths on paper in case
one day someone forgets
who she is or needs

to find her. I'd been waiting
for something like that:
the right side of my face
stained into a kind of proof.

When my husband released
my neck, I turned my other cheek
into the mask of color,

offering my cracked overture,
the vow I'd had all along:
I am who I say I am.
I will come
when my name is called.

FIRST ANNIVERSARY

The newscaster beauty queen demands we evacuate
but I am stunned by her white throat,

the wet vessel that warns me of water rising,
roads blocked, loss of power.

I check that my husband isn't watching me
before I put my hand to the warmth of her

screen. In this wind, she is a marionette,
knees buckling on the sea wall.

I wish she'd fall into my arms.
I wish I'd fall into the ocean. I wish we'd fall

through a looking glass and resurface
on the other side of the world. In our kitchen,

I hear my husband mutter to himself
as he unbinds my dried wedding bouquet,

reassembles the roses so the red blooms pulse
in the center and the white ones stand their guard.

Now the bouquet looks like my heart
if my heart were cut out and brought to him, cradled

on the one copy of our marriage license we keep
in the safe. He winds twine around the stems and hangs

his design above the oven. Has it done something wrong?
My husband flicks the bottom of the stems like he seeks

confessions. Did I know he could tie knots this well?
Are we in flight? Are we the storm? Must we take cover?

He unearths my wedding dress from its quiet tomb
and dissects every hem. The gown is now a series of shelters,

the beads rippling with light like an ocean. He makes me
lie down, his face twisting like he's trying to loosen a seed

from his teeth. He stretches the lace across the gulf
of my body, nails the edges of the dress into the hardwoods

until my wedding ring tightens. May I always be anchored
by the gown I wore when I swore I'd be faithful.

A MORE SUBTLE ACHE

If I'm honest, there is
a place in this body
where a girl won't grow.

When I tilt my head, the row
of white plastic tests
along my mahogany dresser
is a line of little soldiers.
They deny they love this war.

The children I imagined
fled for refuge. Their cribs
groan through the night
but my garden is voiceless,

my general asleep on his back
in the soil where jasmine
used to vine, seep milky sap.
His tongue is sour
when I try to make peace.

My bedroom window holds
no hopeful version of myself,
looking out to the yard
while behind my back
I tie perfect knots

of apron strings, dream
of daughters to carry
the crook of my nose
to the next generation.
My laughter.
My cackle.

This window bears
not the tragedy of a brick
sunk between its panes
but a more subtle ache—

a seal come away
from the glass,
a division
that the enemy
won't even notice.

RITUAL

"Sure, I wanted to believe violence was a little bell
you could ring and get what you wanted."
Carrie Fountain, "Experience" -*Burn Lake*

Every Sunday that summer, my mother dragged me to the heat
of the brick and mortar pet store to buy the bones of other beings.

There was certainty in the ritual. The plastic bag of marrow was always
four dollars, and it always hung rhythmically from my mother's wrist
as we strolled across the parking lot, the bell on the shop's door always

about to stop ringing behind us. Once, my mother spotted a baby
through the fogged window of a stranger's Buick. Alone. Swaddled
in a yellow blanket, the satin hem across its mouth as if to say,

"Keep your hands to yourself." In the nearby pay phone, our coin
clicked into its obedient head. Within an hour, my mother was a hero.

I was too young to know, but I asked why. My mother wouldn't tell me
and the police wouldn't tell me and the store owner slipped behind
the employee-only door with a dead canary, a yellow feather caught

in her hangnail. In the road's crushed gravel, I saw silver.
Like what a woman cinches on her wrists for a ceremony.
Now every summer another news reporter tells a similar story

about a baby found in a suburban parking lot. Each time
I imagine a beautiful woman dismissing motherhood
with ease, shedding it from her body like an endless scarf

with blood hounds vying through the silk, the flash of their teeth
falling away from her collarbone and now nothing can touch her.

I HAVE BEEN EVERYTHING IN THE FAIRY TALE
EXCEPT THE KING AND THE PRINCE

Some nights I am the slice of wedding cake untouched
on the feast table, unable to attract an open mouth.

Some nights I cast curses onto the boy.
If I light a single candle, I find myself in smoke
inside an ornate mirror, ready to counsel stepmothers.

And I am the apple too, seedless and stained
by bitter poison. I am the teeth that bite down.

Some nights I strain like the white horse who yearns
for a quest in the next kingdom. My body is angled
as a wedding invitation waiting for an answer.

My hair is a banner flying. My throat holds
every trumpet, announces royal visitors. And I am

the mercurial glimmer in the mote around this
household. I keep intruders out. I drown them.

When my men are fast asleep, I hold torches,
watch over their doors where I know they are already

dreaming of the flint sparks inside my body,
how my hips will get us to the end of the story
where we'll find the kings I said I'd make them.

LABOR

FAMILY PORTRAIT WITH MY STEPSON'S HEEL
AGAINST MY STOMACH

The morning I first met you, I knelt
before your feet, little god.

Your hands were wild
with the mystery
of tying your own shoes—
a demand for something
that would last.

You memorized the rhymes
to guide yourself,
but you fell to pieces
inside the songs of your parents.

Your heart was the only knot.
A labor pain. I sang, *Build*
a teepee, come inside,
close it tight, so we can hide.

What could I offer but lessons
about building your own shelter?

My boy, you were given worlds
more stirring than my body but you
kicked that one foot toward me.

LABOR DAY WEEKEND AT CAPTIVA ISLAND

As the beach town hushed
down to sleep, I ran
hot water over white dishes

and watched the boy
through the window as he broke
for the end of the dock
where his father dropped
a hook into a calm ocean.

The sea was so pale
that it was possible then,
even through the green
heaving chest of water,
to see to the bottom.

Fish rose to the child
with their sore mouths
going open and open

and I wondered:
How does the boy
view my origin?
At what moment
did I become his?

Was I the fresh lumber
for the part of the dock
that was missing?

Was I the oyster shell
that sliced his heel
in the slap of the salt water?

Was I the balm
his father soothed across the cut
and then wiped from his hands
with a rough red towel?

He ran a finger
over the wood's blond dust
and slipped it in his mouth
so he might know what it is.

FAMILY PORTRAIT AT THE NEIGHBORHOOD POOL

When did that row of foliage
become a line of guards
with their gaze tilted at the knots
in my green bikini? My smile

fills the heart
of the sago palm
with alarm. She grows

nervous, shivers
her thousand needles
to brush the cheek
of the withered bird of paradise

who raises her startled beak
and nods to the jasmine,
cueing her to snake through

the chain link fence,
border the rules
of the neighborhood

pool. The boy flares red
as a slice of setting sun,
disappears
under the water

and the world of leaves
readies itself
for whatever harm
a stepmother can do
to another woman's child.

THE FLOWERS BETWEEN OUR HOUSES
WON'T STOP SWELLING

When I trade my stepson back —
the canna flowers —
that hide his mother's house —
move like magic tricks —

their stems —
a row of wands —
aubergine and —
eight feet tall —

his mother watches —
through a thick curtain —
on the other side —
as the boy and I part —
flowers with our forearms —

and the door to her house —
appears every time —
the wood refusing —
to seal up for good —

this —
it's my most —
failing —
abracadabra —

and the blooms are quick —
when they flash their silk—
handkerchiefs —
convincingly dyed —
red and limp and brilliant —
above my head —

the door closes behind him —
with a hush —
whispering a spell —
to make a woman —
split in half —

IN MY PAPER GOWN I PRESS MY MOUTH
AGAINST THE WINDOW

In the orchard beyond this hospital, citrus falls
        into the hands of the innocent. A boy and a girl race through

           the gnarled rows, plastic grocery bags rattling like flags
    around their perfect wrists. Like marriage, this is a game.

When they walk out of the orchard with their glowing treasures,
        one orange globe goes missing behind the girl,

           a bright history soon to be sunken in— and swarmed.

A STEPMOTHER WONDERS AT A BOY
NOT MADE OF IVORY

The boy says, *Wait*— in the middle of the museum, among all that
cold stone. The boy wants to know how many seconds
we have been alive. And so we sit, legs crossed toward each other
while, behind his precious head, a great king's son lounges
in ivory. How lucky we are not to be art— cast into roles
we cannot mold or reverse. In the dim light of the museum,
we pencil erasable numbers on the back of a business card
I excavate from the dust of mints in the depths of my purse.
We calculate each breath, each sword clash, each morning
when we could wake and dream up any other possible life.

THE PLAYGROUND WHERE I TAKE THE BOY
WHEN I CAN'T SLEEP

It isn't any less frightening
that the lion's head
that holds my stepson is plastic.

It's a replica of an animal,
as surely I am a replica
of a mother. The child
invites me inside
the mouth that never closes.

He is drawn
to graffiti scrawled all along
the great hinge of the lion's jaw.
He begs, "Read it to me!"

I lean into the shadowed cave,
but the nightmare scribble
that exists where teeth should be
is a line from Peter Pan,

spoken in a land where no one
grows up. I trace his finger
over the faded letters, whisper,
"To die would be an awfully
big adventure." I strain

to read the words, faded
as though a new mother
wrote them but returned

with bitter astringent, raised
her soaked cloth to the lion's mouth
and decided to live for a child.

RED GERANIUMS

If you don't already know their scent,
I can't tell you. But who among us can
describe our mother's musk
on a day when she has yet to bathe?

*

In the soil of my childhood,
my mother planted a garden
but refused to let me help her.

I watched her kneel to the earth,
wondering why she thought
I might steal her chance at burying
a seed in her own wet darkness.

She wanted to make things
struggle into beauty.
Was I not enough?

*

She repeated this process
every spring, then returned
to bed for the rest of the year.

One day I stepped into her garden
and laid down, submitting
to the row of red geraniums.
I have never belonged to anything

like I belong to her.
Are we not all
looking for a cure
for the thing we love
which has been torn apart?

*

I beheaded
every living flower,
climbed to the top
of the slick stairs

and lay the blooms
so that their faces
faced her. Her chin,
her ribs, her hips, her knees
and the feet she used

to stomp in that same room,
right before I came
into the world, splitting her open
as she begged for me to stop.

WHY SHOULD I PLANT THAT
WHEN I KNOW IT WON'T LAST?

The boy grows older without my permission.
The seconds he and I have left to live
in this brick house where we found each other

sift from my body like the powder that keeps my face
from reflecting God. He is the white dust that drifts,
particle by particle, from my eyelids, my temples.

I hardly notice the ivory flurry; most days I just bury us
in domestic lists and their crosses, the routes we need to take.
By nightfall, my cheeks shiver with shine. I submerge

in the bath's quiet singe, cover my eyes with my palms.
But what does it matter? The magic of his boyhood
is a light ash landing where I step out of scalding water
and have no choice but to praise his holy name and let him fall.

THINGS I HAVE SAID TO THE RED ROSES
HIS FIRST WIFE PLANTED

A good flood
could bury
your beauty.

I will grant you
one favor, but not
one more than that.

I will set the ladder
outside of your life
and watch you
from the top step.

There is not a word,
a wave, a shiver
that divides your petals
that I will not see.

Aren't you
a gorgeous
little sinner?

Aren't I
your merciful
God?

WHAT I WANT THEM TO SAY ABOUT ME
THE NEXT TIME I LOSE A BABY

1. The first wife should say,

> If you placed
> a sheet of white paper
> into a bathtub of scald,
>
> and from the marble edge
> you sang the length
> of the alphabet
> before slipping
> the paper out
>
> and expecting it
> to beat a man
> in a wrestling match,
>
> the result would be
> this woman, here.

2. The sisters should say,

> It's simple.
> She is tired from shifting
> between each of the wives
> she is supposed to become:
>
> the grief counselor,
> the washer of others' hands,
> the translator
>
> of dictionaries, the voice
> of reason, the knife
> through every apple,
> her blade sharpened always,

her glare too beautiful
when it's drowned

in a juice that sets
our hearts racing
when she winces.

3. The stepson should say,

I bring her
sweet coffee
every morning
but she never
touches it.

I am the one
who gets to cut flowers,
who fills crystal vases
with clean water.

I am super quiet
when I place them
on her nightstand,
when she's sleeping

which is always.
I whisper
to the blooms,
"Do not to worry.
She dreams of us."

4. The mother should say,

What's anyone
supposed to do
with her story?

Why won't this town just
let her lie down
in a bed of white sheets,
coverlets pulled up

around her neck
by a decent doctor now.

A good pillow
under her head would let
her dreams alone.

5. The neighbor should say,

Who was this woman
before she became a tangle
of everyone else's needs?

In my fantasy for her,
she can't even read.

We can't trust her
to hold so much
as a glass of water.

We have to tell her
if she'll need a jacket
to go outside.

Let her never empire,
never white silk, never
be moonstruck, let her
never leap year,
never one-way.

Let every theater
she enters
have the spotlights
switched off. Let
the bulbs break.

6. The husband should say,

Has she slept since
I broke our bedroom
door down

and found her
on the floor with blood
in her nightgown?

That cracked door
leaned on our garage
for a week before
it was taken away.

Who knows now
where that gold
doorknob turns?

To what
does that door open
now that she
is always closed?

THE BEDROOM IS A LABYRINTH I AM LOST INSIDE

I need instructions on how to open again.

Like a woman made of expertly folded maps sewn together,
       my husband's first wife appears on the edge of the labyrinth

with familiar advice: *Lie back and think of a rose garden.*

When she pantomimes the instruction, "lie back,"
       her body makes a sound like an urgent man

ripping open a delicate envelope with his thumb. Inside her

is the most beautiful invitation— intact and on linen, her address in gold.
       The curve of each letter loops back to its rightful owner.

If you so much as hesitate, she warns, *he'll come hunting for me.*

With ease, she slides through the glisten of a hedge
       I didn't even know was parted. I hide

in the curved belly of an unnamed fountain, drained. Still,
       my husband finds me, lifts me out, and cleans red algae

from my fingernails. Everyone has something to say about how to
       get over it, but my husband, every time he touches me, is all thorns.

THE MASTER BATHROOM RENOVATION

We decided to undress / on the other side of the house / our bathtub suffering a nervous Victorian ruin / apprehensive as a young wife hiding / her breasts as she changes her blouse / The first time it was an accident / my damp lace left on the floor / and the workers afraid / to go near it / A week later / the wet paint dizzied the beginning of our marriage / and I left tokens for the men / I planted them / as my husband slept / My first was the fogged crucifix necklace / Mother bought me when I began / to bleed / The day they removed our pink marble sink and laid its cupped body / in a corner / I listened for signs / of their discovery as the pure gold chain / snaked in the shower drain / The body of Christ glared at the rusted razorblade / I offered the next day / And then the unopened bottle of diet pills / the diary from twelfth grade / the inherited diamond broach Daddy bought for his own private and glittering restoration / like a fistful of light to stab over a woman's heart / It was no accident / the workers wading through dust and / the white tiles / and the black tiles / and the light bulbs / electrified among the parts of myself that I left for the men to repair.

SPLINTER

THINGS I HAVE SAID TO MY HUSBAND
OR
THE GRIEF OF A WOODEN FENCE IN A FIELD

I can't stop you
from climbing over me.

Do you even pause
to consider why
another man buried
my feet in this earth?
Where are you going
that's so wonderful?

I feel your fingers grasp
the knots in my limbs.
I bend under the weight
of your leather boot.

I rise stronger as you leap
into the air, land
in a kneeling position.
When you close your eyes,
who is behind those lids?

Some men find me
irresistible. Others
have broken bones
trying to steady themselves
on top of me.

To whose open arms
does your path take you? You,
who rub your cracked palms
together not to pray for us
but to wipe off the dust
I left on your hands.

A HUSBAND EAVESDROPS AS HIS WIFE CONFIDES
IN A BOX OF MATCHES

For God is not the author of confusion...
1 Corinthians 14:33

Some nights I can't remember what I've promised him.
Some nights I cannot speak at all.
How long will it take to convince him
that my mouth is not an open dictionary?

Some nights I cannot speak at all.
I cannot go more than three days
with a dictionary of prayer in my open mouth.
He will need to build me a room where I can be alone.

I cannot go more than three days
without longing for my father, the fire wrangler.
Maybe he could build me a room where I can be alone
with the memory of my mother, who sold diamonds

while she longed for my father and for fire and for danger.
The light in the store made her look younger.
I don't have memories of the diamonds my mother sold
before her house burned to the ground.

Did the light of that fire make her look younger?
I oil my forehead and cheeks before I sleep.
Who burned their house to the ground?
Will my husband be wise enough to hide his matches?

I anoint my forehead and cheeks before I sleep.
There are things I doubt my God will forgive.
Will my husband be wise enough to hide his matches?
He will need to find a way to bring my Florida back.

There are things I doubt my God will forgive.
What is the remedy for escaping an enclosed space?
I will find a way to bring my Florida back.
I will become the perfect wife. I make dull things bright.

WHEN STRANGERS ASK, "DON'T YOU WANT ANY REAL CHILDREN?"

For a decade
I have been polite as
first holy communion gloves.

Now I no longer care
to live under the glass
of this question.

There is no longer
a galaxy beneath my skirt
to photograph, no longer
a doctor scrawling out
solutions for
Mrs. Better Half.

My medicine cabinet holds
no rows of syringes
for my husband
to play darts with.

I am no longer bent over.
I am no longer a body
of dried berries.

My kin have a lineage
of twins and triplets.
We are award-winning for it,

our dinner tables so large
they must be carved from ancient trees.
When we feast, we feast like dogs.
It takes extra men to move
our furniture when we leave.

My sleep will never be interrupted.
I am deaf to all clocks going mad
with pendulum alarms, calling
me when I float down the street
when I am late to pick up no one.

IN MY WEDDING HEELS, I BUY
FROZEN BLACKBERRIES FOR A PIE

Whose fingerprints
stamped their slick on this
aisle's frosted window?

These oily labyrinths
could belong to any hand—
why not a man who could
make me give all this up?

Outside town, a man digs
a shovel into the shimmer
of coal until a train unclenches
from whatever was keeping it
from racing through a country.

MY HUSBAND BURNS MY CLOTHES IN THE DRIVEWAY

Even my wedding dress. Even my tights after he scissored
        the crook out of them. Even my running shoes.

A year ago, my husband made a terrible joke
        about what he'd do if he found out I kissed another man.

I had permission to tongue all the neighborhood women
        I could convince to want me, but no part of a man's body

was to cross the threshold of my mouth. I stayed devoted
        for an eternity. When tempted, I'd go for long walks

through the grocery store that faces our house. I'd caress
        containers of dried apricots, wonder where their water is now.

Does it rest quietly in the bucket of roses a man buys for his mistress?
        Might it be used to one day douse a promised flame?

In every aisle, I gripped my list and followed the man in the red apron
        who screwed jars of preserves tighter, counted a chorus line of vinegar bottles.

I watched as he pulled apart celery stalks and collapsed cardboard boxes
        under his heels. I watched as he rotated rotten apples

to hide their bruises. When the spray of water misted onto the lush he lorded over,
        he never even flinched. But neither did I that day when he finally

extended his hand toward my lips with a sample. A blackberry
        warmed by his palm. Little honeycomb, his darkened, sour heart.

I parted my mouth like my mother taught me. Like my priest taught me. Like my
        husband taught me. I returned home to a blaze writhing on the concrete

with laughter. My husband said he was surprised by how easily my clothes
        ignited. Some punchline. Turns out, I was flammable all along.

CONTEMPLATING AN AFFAIR

A mile from the shore,
the firefighters find
all the pretty horses
stuck in the fences they nuzzled
their enormous heads against
through the first years
of our marriage. Drowned
by this sudden flash
of water, they are now just like
the mute figurines
I used to mess with
as a girl. If I wanted it to be,
my house was a graveyard
of horses. Horses upside down
in the fireplace, rearing.
Horses hidden deep
in the boots of my father,
galloping. Horses holding
their breath in the water
I poured into a blender.
No. I never flicked
the switch. Not with
those looks they gave me
when they came up for air.

DOUBLE-BLIND

In the ordered lush of the new grocery store, I dreamt of groves
    of men unable to walk, calling my name chorus-like,

        crippled in rows by the thought of me
unbuttoning an orange silk blouse. Sipping their bitter juice.

When I returned home hours later, my husband had painted the bathroom
    to match my hair color. A temple of blonde where he could beg

        my forgiveness. I blended in to that tiny chamber,
my pallor highlighted like a target. How is it, then, that he still misses me?

A HUSBAND DARES HIS WIFE TO HAVE AN AFFAIR

I let him stage me
in the emerald outfit
he bought for the occasion.

It was August.
I nearly wrecked
the dress with sweat.

It took an hour
for his hands to secure
each pearl button
from my waist
to the nape of my neck.

When he was done,
I was ripe
as the garden of Eden.
My throat had never
been more open.

He ordered me a taxi
headed for the beach hotel where,
one summer as a child,
I was pulled under by the tide.

I felt mesmerized
by the silk across my thighs—
its animal origin,
human destination.

I whispered to the driver,
"You can't live forever.
You can't live forever."

When I arrived,
my wedding heels crushed
the mint carpet of the lobby.

I ordered bourbon at the hotel bar,
sipped its amber heat
until the silk around my ribs
darkened. I grew

heavier. And slower.
When I tried to stand
the dress clung to my body,
snaking between my legs.

Men in suits looked up
from glossy menus,
loosened their ties.

I tried to convince myself
I was any other animal,
unbound by buttons,
unstained by rouge,
and running,

but when I looked down
at the leather suitcase
my husband packed me,
the fever of my daring
failed. I could not viper.
I could not devil.
I am no Eve.

What I might be
is the opposite of the apple:
the other spouse, alone
in the last moments
of the garden, suspecting
nothing of his mate.

MY HUSBAND BRINGS HOME A TERRARIUM

His gift dared me to lift its lid.
When I did, the unlocked swamp
cast off its fever, a hot breath
metallic as the gold doorknobs

of Espiritu Santo Church,
so hot they could disappear
fingerprints if you lingered,
unsure about your own burning.

But then the scent shifted deeper,
a scene before Sunday mass
when one of the Dewberry boys
whose blonde hair shined

like the cloth across Christ's waxy hips
put his lips to my pierced ear
and whispered that I had a voice
like deep fried barbed wire.

I pulled my knees to my chest
and temper-kicked the hymnals
in front of me, stamping
my white patent leather shoes
into all those prayers bound
by the most desperate believers.

The dirt caked on my Mary Jane's
fell to the marble floor, settled
in the shade of that humid world
under a church pew in the South,

beneath the rust-scented sins
of local husbands and wives
who hide their secrets behind
cans of Aqua Net and razorblades.

Where is that dirt now?
And is it in fact like love
in that it can never disappear?

MY HUSBAND'S SLEEP

My husband's sleep is heavy as the rusted trucks that moan
      when the city pulls them off the beach after a storm.

It comes fast as the flash floods that wash order from our streets, turn
      the public library to a swamp of spines, a wrecked terrarium

where stories we once tucked into their covers tremble an alphanumeric blur.
      I study my husband as he breathes one deep sigh and drifts off.

He is lavender water receding from the shore of my day. His silhouette echoes
      his Sarasota father who loved him best with a closed fist

when he refused to bathe as a child. In my husband's sleep is the fear of drowning.
      His mother's meticulous chore board. Gold stars. Dust on his swim medals

and the diplomas under his childhood bed. In his sleep is his son's birth certificate,
      the lock of hair from that first haircut, its sweet curl held by a blue ribbon.

In his sleep is the font on his first marriage license. His lawyer's leather wallet. The scent
      of nutmeg at Christmas and cologne on New Year's Eve. After midnight

in his sleep, his annotated Bible whispers the verses he wishes he could memorize
      as easily as our rose bush memorizes its thorns. In his sleep, he aches

with impatience like a tied-down horse. Twitching behind his eyelids
      are all the women he might have loved but didn't, squalls broken

on another coast. I've never seen a man as beautiful as he is. I am
      a seawall drowned by this husband. In my sleep, there is only him.

WE GAVE OURSELVES THE SUMMER TO FIND THE SPARK

With a paring knife, my husband slit a serrano open.

I swore I couldn't do it, but he held the back of my head in his palm
and made me stick my tongue inside its seeded folds

until my bare feet stamped the cold tile. Like a good wife,
I did the same for him, proudly counting all those seconds

he held it longer, my silk slip sticking to my back as I laughed
with a tongue that could have burned our house down.

And they too were riven in half, the bad girls
in the horror films I made him binge that summer.

They stood no chance as they scurried down basement stairs,
their delicate ankles twisting just off-screen, pianos in high alert.

My husband pierced wet chunks of pineapple with skewers and laid them
like virgins in rows on an open flame until they hissed at us.

Their smoke was sweet, blew ashes into my undone hair.
Under the night sky, I plucked diamonds out of the bracelet

my father gave my mother the first time he slept with another woman.
I glued them to my legs until I became a joke of a constellation.

On the 4th of July, I sat on the edge of the sink and took a blade
to my husband's beard. He turned back into the boy

who knew nothing about me but my name. I kissed
the strange young soldier and buried his hair in a wastebasket.

Outside, light exploded for all the children we never had.

One morning, we cleaned up nice and went to confession
at Our Lady of Lourdes. Our sins were difficult

to explain, our penances so hard to complete we suspected
they were meant to banish us. Father Xavier made us hold incense smoke

in our mouths. For days, our vision was blurry and we coughed dust
into our coffee every morning, but we did try to change.

Yet by August we were inventing new curse words. I graffitied them
on the fence that surrounds his ex-wife's neighborhood while he stood

guard, ready with the whistle. When we got home, he said we should plan
for our deaths. We wrote a will on the back of a light bill. Our ashes

are to be sprinkled in the backyard where he proposed to me,
near the roots of the twisted wisteria vines that my husband beats

with a broomstick to make it believe it's dying,
to shock it into reproducing, make it burst a brighter bloom.

ACKNOWLEDGMENTS

Grateful acknowledgment is due to the editors of the following journals and anthologies where poems from this collection first appeared.

AGNI: "A Stepmother Wonders at a Boy Not Made of Ivory"

Bear Review: "Labor Day Weekend at Captiva Island"

Eckerd Review: "Where My Mind Went During the First Ultrasound"

Pigment from the Past / It Never Dries: An Anthology of Contemporary Self-Elegies and Essays (forthcoming): "The Bedroom is a Labyrinth I am Lost Inside," "Terrarium"

Silk Road: "The Game of Make-Believe," "The Ever After Bridal Store," "The Rented Altar," "Honeymoon Island," "My Husband's Sleep"

Spark and Echo: "A Husband Eavesdrops as His Wife Confides in a Box of Matches," "What I Want Them to Say About Me the Next Time I Lose Another Baby"

The Adroit Journal: "The Master Bathroom Renovation"

The Dead Animal Handbook: "Ritual"

The Journal: "White Picket Fence and Black Coffee"

The White Wall Review: "Red Geraniums" and "I Have Been Everything in the Fairy Tale Except the King and the Prince"

For those whose patient feedback shaped these poems: Hayan Charara, Chelsea B. DesAutels, Niki Herd, Tony Hoagland, Joshua Gottlieb-Miller, Luke Jacob, Brandon Lamson, Faith Padgett, Nancy Reddy, Jan Saenz, Tray Shellberg, Liza Watkins, Tria Wood, and Theodora Ziolkowski.

For those who guided me through the process of bringing my work into the world: Craig Beaven, Erin Belieu, Carrie Fountain, Terrance Hayes, Anna Journey, Tomás Q. Morin, and Laura Van Prooyen.

For those who provided the luxury of time and space to write: Anna Caudle, Emily Baker, and Julie Watkins. I was blessed to borrow your calm, quiet rooms where poems were born with ease.

For every generous light in the Poetry at Round Top community, I am fueled by the warmth of our gathering each April. I am grateful for Naomi Shihab Nye for guiding me to the conference when I first started this manuscript; without you, I would not have found that sacred space at Festival Hill. I am now a better poet and reader because of the time I've spent with Jesse Bertron, Luke Jacob, Judy Jensen, and Katherine Durham Oldmixon. Thanks to all of you for your orchestration of magic each year.

For John Gosslee, my editor at C&R Press, who has placed boundless faith in my work. I am in awe of how much you encourage my vision. Thank you and everyone at C&R Press for helping me realize the dream of this collection.

And for Tray. Always for Tray. You have helped me build a life where my art can thrive.

C&R PRESS TITLES

NONFICTION

Women in the Literary Landscape by Doris Weatherford, et al
Credo: An Anthology of Manifestos & Sourcebook for Creative
Writing by Rita Banerjee and Diana Norma Szokolyai

FICTION

Last Tower to Heaven by Jacob Paul
History of the Cat in Nine Chapters or Less by Anis Shivani
No Good, Very Bad Asian by Lelund Cheuk
Surrendering Appomattox by Jacob M. Appel
Made by Mary by Laura Catherine Brown
Ivy vs. Dogg by Brian Leung
While You Were Gone by Sybil Baker
Cloud Diary by Steve Mitchell
Spectrum by Martin Ott
That Man in Our Lives by Xu Xi

SHORT FICTION

Fathers of Cambodian Time-Travel Science by Bradley Bazzle
Two Californias by Robert Glick
Notes From the Mother Tongue by An Tran
The Protester Has Been Released by Janet Sarbanes

ESSAY AND CREATIVE NONFICTION

Selling the Farm by Debra Di Blasi
the internet is for real by Chris Campanioni
In the Room of Persistent Sorry by Kristina Marie Darling
Immigration Essays by Sybil Baker
Je suis l'autre: Essays and Interrogations
by Kristina Marie Darling
Death of Art by Chris Campanioni

POETRY

9 781949 540147